Whale Sharks

BY ALLAN MOREY

D0700320

AMICUS HIGH INTEREST • AMICUS INK

Amicus High Interest and Amicus Ink are imprints of Amicus
P.O. Box 1329, Mankato, MN 56002
www.amicuspublishing.us

Library of Congress Cataloging-in-Publication Data
Names: Morey, Allan, author.
Title: Whale sharks / by Allan Morey.
Description: Mankato, MN : Amicus High Interest, [2017] |
 Series: Sharks | Audience: K to grade 3._ | Includes index.
Identifiers: LCCN 2015033753 (print) | LCCN 2015041758
 (ebook) | ISBN 9781607539810 (library binding) | ISBN
 9781681520940 (pbk.) | ISBN 9781681510156 (ebook)
 | ISBN 9781681510156 (pdf)
Subjects: LCSH: Whale shark–Juvenile literature.
Classification: LCC QL638.95.R4 M67 2017 (print) | LCC
 QL638.95.R4 (ebook) | DDC 597.3/3–dc23
LC record available at http://lccn.loc.gov/2015033753

Editor: Wendy Dieker
Series Designer: Kathleen Petelinsek
Book Designer: Aubrey Harper
Photo Researchers: Rebecca Bernin & Aubrey Harper

Photo Credits: National Geographic/Superstock cover;
Reinhard Dirscherl/age fotostock Spain S.L./Corbis 5; Brian
J. Skerry/National Geographic Creative 6; nicolas.voisin44/
Shutterstock 8-9; Reinhard Dirscherl/Alamy Stock Photo 10;
Nature Picture Library/Alamy Stock Photo 13; Lebendkulturen
de/Shutterstock 14; paul cowell photography/Getty 17;
torstenvelden/RooM the Agency/Corbis 18; Suzanne Long/
Alamy Stock Photo 21; richcarey/iStock 22; eyalcohen/
iStock 24-25; Reinhard Dirscherl/Alamy Stock Photo 26; Soren
Egeberg Photography/Shutterstock 29

Printed in the United States of America.

HC 10 9 8 7 6 5 4 3 2 1
PB 10 9 8 7 6 5 4 3 2 1

Table of Contents

A Giant Fish

Small fish swim around in the ocean. Jellyfish bob up and down. Tiny squid dart through the water. But watch out! Huge fish also lurk nearby. A large shadow moves toward the smaller animals. They try to swim away. But they can't. Like a big vacuum, a whale shark sucks the tiny fish into its mouth. Gulp!

The gaping mouth of this whale shark sucks in small fish.

Whale sharks are the largest fish in the ocean.

 How big do whale sharks grow?

Do not let its name fool you. A whale shark is not a whale. It's a whale-sized shark. Whale sharks are the world's largest fish. They can grow to be as long as a school bus. And they are heavy, too. **Adult** whale sharks weigh more than a school bus full of kids.

 Very big! They grow up to 40 feet (12 m) long.

The "shark" part of their name is not tricky. These giant fish are sharks. But they are not like most other sharks. While big, they aren't scary killers. They don't have rows of long, sharp teeth. They don't chomp and gnash. Whale sharks are peaceful animals. They slowly glide through the water. People can even swim alongside them.

Divers swim with this gentle giant.

Whale sharks feed on small fish and tiny plants and animals that are too small to see.

Filter Feeders

Like all sharks, whale sharks eat other animals. They are **predators**. These fish may be huge. And they may have a giant mouth. But they eat the smallest animals in the ocean. They eat lots and lots of **zooplankton**. Many of these tiny animals are too small to see.

How does a whale shark eat these tiny animals? Whale sharks are **filter feeders**. They suck water filled with tiny fish into their mouths. Then they push the water out through their **gills**. The gills are covered with pads that have tiny holes. These pads catch and trap the food in the water. Then the whale sharks swallow. Yum!

 Are any other sharks filter feeders?

Whale sharks have gills that are long and wide.

Yes! Basking sharks and the megamouth

We need a microscope to see these plankton. The very biggest are only 0.2 inches (5 mm) long.

 Does a whale shark ever suck up bigger animals?

Whale sharks are not the only animals that eat zooplankton. Many kinds of small animals also feed on these tiny creatures. As a whale shark sucks up water, it catches these animals too. Whale sharks will eat small squids, crabs, and jellyfish. As long as the food is small enough, it will be swallowed.

 Sometimes. But a whale shark has a narrow throat. It can't swallow big animals. It will spit them out.

Life Cycle

Whale sharks are loners. So not much is known about how they mate. People do not often see more than one at a time. But scientists do know they give live birth to their young. Young sharks are called **pups**. A female whale shark gives birth to about 300 pups.

Two whale sharks are not often
seen together. But they do come
together to mate.

This spotted whale shark was born ready to survive on its own.

 How long do whale sharks live?

A young whale shark looks like an adult, only it is much smaller. A pup is around 2 feet (60 cm) long. Pups have spots on their backs just like adults do. Whale sharks grow slowly. Scientists believe they become adults at about 30 years old.

 A long time! Some live up to 100 years.

Life in the Ocean

Whale sharks like warm water. So they stay in tropical areas. These places are near the **equator**. Whale sharks live in the northern Indian Ocean. They also swim in parts of the Pacific and Atlantic Oceans. In the spring, many whale sharks **migrate**. They swim to the west coast of Australia. There they can find lots of food.

Whale sharks are sometimes seen in the Ningaloo Reef Marine Park in Australia.

Water filled with tiny plants and animals gets pulled into the huge whale shark's mouth.

 Q How much food does a whale shark eat?

Whale sharks are big and slow. No other animal hunts them, so they do not need to swim fast to escape predators. Actually, they do not really need to move at all. Other filter feeders swim to draw water into their mouths. But whale sharks suck up water like a vacuum. This is how they catch food.

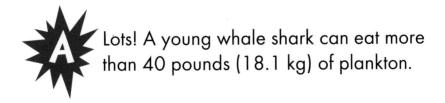 Lots! A young whale shark can eat more than 40 pounds (18.1 kg) of plankton.

Like many fish, whale sharks have a darker back and lighter belly. Their dark back can be brown, gray, or blue. Whale sharks also have spots on their backs and bellies. These spots are special. Each whale shark has a different pattern. Scientists can tell whale sharks apart by their spots.

The spots on a whale shark are like fingerprints. Each whale has a unique pattern.

Fishers see a whale shark swim under their platform. What a sight!

Sharks and People

Whale sharks are not a threat to people. They cannot eat large prey. But people can cause much harm to whale sharks. These fish feed near the surface of the water. A passing ship or boat could hit one. Oil spills can cause trouble too. The shark might pull oil from the water through its gills. That can make it sick.

People also hunt whale sharks. They use shark fins to make soup. They use shark liver oil for medicines. Some governments are working to save whale sharks. They have laws making it a crime to catch them. Australia even created an ocean park. Whale sharks swim safely through water at the Ningaloo Reef Marine Park.

Laws that protect whale sharks help make sure people can swim with them for years to come.

Glossary

adult A fully grown animal.

equator An imaginary line around the middle of the Earth.

filter feeder An animal that eats by passing water filled with tiny plants and animals over a body part that traps the food.

gills Openings on the sides of a fish; fish use gills for breathing, but whale sharks also use them to filter tiny animals from the water.

migrate To move from one area to another in search of food.

predator An animal that hunts other animals.

pup A young shark.

zooplankton Very small animals that live in water.

Read More

LeBreton, Sue. *Whale Shark*. New York: AV2 by Weigl, 2015.

Meister, Cari. *Do You Really Want to Meet a Shark?* Mankato, Minn: Amicus, 2016.

Musgrave, Ruth. *National Geographic Kids Everything Sharks*. Washington, D.C.: National Geographic, 2011.

Websites

A-Z Animals—Whale Sharks
a-z-animals.com/animals/whale-shark

National Geographic—Whale Shark
animals.nationalgeographic.com/animals/fish/whale-shark

World Wildlife Fund—Whale Sharks
www.worldwildlife.org/species/whale-shark

Index

About the Author

Allan Morey is a children's book author and lover of animals, both big and small. He's had pet fish, birds, ferrets, pigs, cats, and dogs. Animals are one of his favorite subjects to write about. He now lives in St. Paul, Minnesota, with his wife, two kids, and dog, Ty.